MW01689698

For Steve

my fri[illegible]

fellow pastor

[illegible]

3/01

INPSYTE

The Power of Opposite Strengths

By Jay Thomas, Ed.D.

Copyright © INPSYTE 1998
All rights reserved.

Printed in the United States of America
by New Forums Press, Inc., P.O. Box 876,
Stillwater, OK 74076.

ISBN: 1-58107-005-5

Insight

The ability to see and understand clearly the inner nature of things.

Webster's New World Dictionary

Inpsyte

The ability to see and understand clearly the inner nature of people.

What This Book Is About

This book is about understanding yourself and your relationships. It is a practical, hands-on, how-to book. You gain insight into yourself and see what you need to do to solve your relationship problems.

You can expect these benefits:

Knowing yourself - who you really are at the core of your Being

The Thomas Concept gives us the means to describe eight *Patterns of Strengths*. You are guided to identify your own pattern. Your pattern gives you insight into who you really are – at the core.

Learning how to use your strengths to become the person you want to be

Your strengths come in pairs. We tend to use only one strength to solve our problems. You learn how to solve your problems by using both strengths.

Knowing others as they really are

You learn to look at others in terms of their strengths. This helps you to see them as they really are – at the core.

Discovering how others see you

You gain insight into why others see you the way they do. These insights give you clear guidance into how to improve your relationships.

Knowing how to solve your relationship problems

You see what is causing your relationship problems. Then, follow step-by-step guidelines in solving them.

TO
Past, Present and Future
Users
Of
The Thomas Concept

Contents

Acknowledgements

This book is a distillation of what I have learned about people. Many people have influenced my thinking. Family, friends, authors, teachers, people with whom I have counseled, students in my seminars, and associates who use *The Thomas Concept* – all have played a part in my education.

I don't know where to start or where to end in naming particular people. So I'll just acknowledge my indebtedness to all. Some know who they are, others have influenced me without ever knowing it.

Creative Strength is Made Up of Opposite Strengths

This insight has historical roots.

The ancient Greeks used the phrase *"Hieros Gamos"* to express it. Translated into English it means "The sacred marriage of opposites." Greek scholars tell us that it is the sacred marriage of their male and female Gods.

Prehistoric Chinese people had the same insight. The traditional Chinese symbol yin/yang is used to express it. It is an important feature of one of their most popular religions – *Taoism.*

The insight came to me in 1962. It happened without awareness of the prior insights. Since then, it has evolved into what is known as *The Thomas Concept.* This book is grounded in this concept.

The Thomas Concept is a way of understanding Creative Strength and how it works in the lives of people.

The Thomas Concept

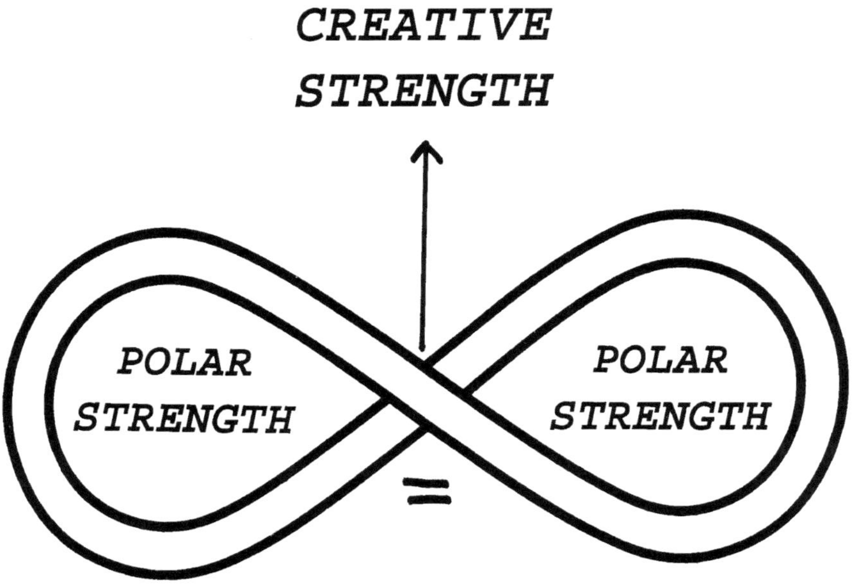

Seven Principles

1. Human strengths come in pairs.
2. The two strengths are opposites.
3. They are equally valuable.
4. The action of one creates a need for the action of the other.
5. They work together to produce <u>Creative Strength.</u>
6. Neither strength is creative by itself.
7. People have more strength in one than the other.

Chapter 1

Your Natural Self

Over 2300 years ago Socrates advised his students to "Know thyself."

In Shakespeare's *Hamlet*, Polonius says,

> "This above all – to thine own self be true,
> And it must follow, as the night the day,
> Thou canst not then be false to any man."

In Arthur Miller's *Death of a Salesman*, Willie Loman's son, standing at the graveside of his father, says, "He never knew who he was."

What are you being true to when you are "being true to yourself?" What are you doing when you are "being yourself?" What is this "true self" that is really you? This chapter is devoted to answering these questions.

What Is Your "Self" Made Of?

Your "Self" is grounded in the physical reality of your body. It is a unique bundle of strengths at the core of your being.

Your self is made up of pure strengths – no weaknesses. We call these strengths "Core Strengths."

Your core strengths come in pairs. The two strengths in each pair are *opposites*. They are polar to one another, like the north and south poles. The individual strengths are called "polar" strengths.

You have three pairs of polar strengths:

(1) A basic pair – **Thinking** and **Risking**
(2) A thinking pair – **Practical thinking** and **Theoretical thinking**
(3) A risking pair – **Out-dependent risking** and **In-dependent risking**

These three pairs of Core Strengths are displayed on page 13.

Three Pairs of Core Strengths

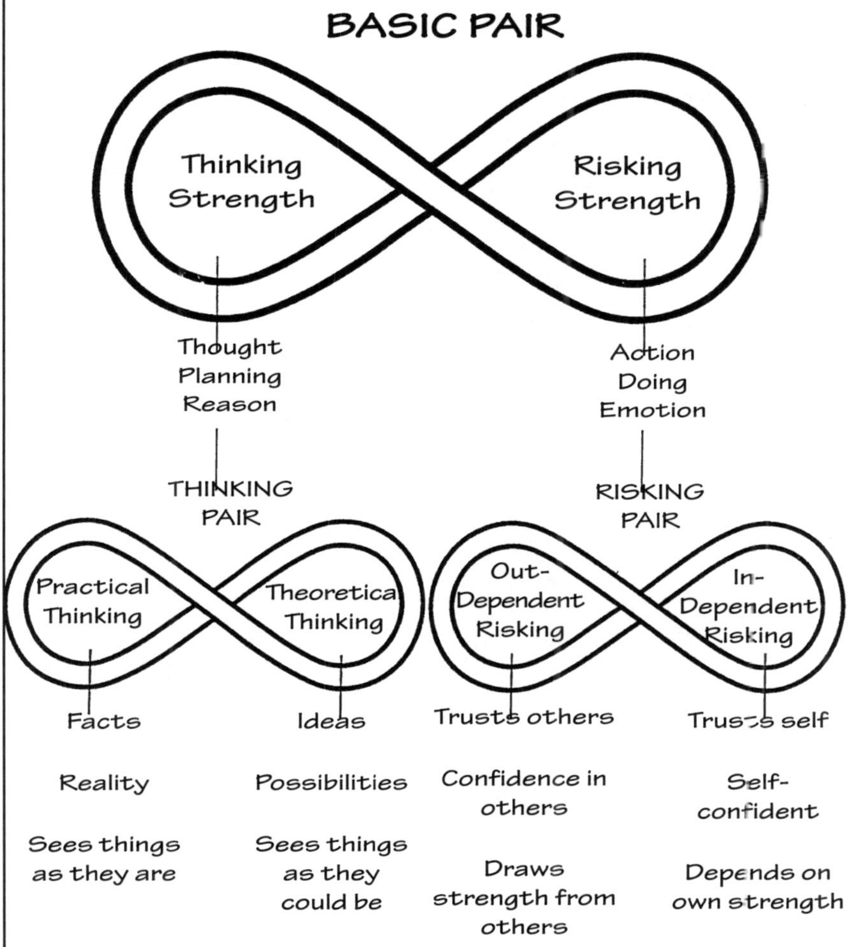

The Basic Pair
Thinking and Risking

reason and emotion - mind and body - head and heart - thought and action

These are common dichotomies used to point towards your two basic strengths. We use the terms *Thinking* and *Risking* to identify these two polar strengths.

We all know about thinking and risking because we use these strengths everyday. We think and feel; we plan and do; we analyze a problem and do something about it.

We see other people expressing the same two strengths. They consider alternatives and make decisions; they determine the odds and take chances; they think about what to do and move into action.

Your thinking strength is a stabilizing strength. It brings order and rationality to your life. Through it you evaluate, weigh, judge and set priorities.

It is your cognitive, reasoning, planning side. Through its' use you visualize goals and develop strategies to reach them.

Your thinking strength gives you an <u>*understanding*</u> *of life.*

On the other hand, your risking strength is a dynamic, action-oriented strength. It is your emotional, feeling side. It is a moving, restless, doing kind of strength – associated with the **heart** or **gut**.

Your risking strength enables you to expose yourself, to move out, to take a chance, to initiate, to be involved, to cause things to happen. It brings excitement, passion, and exhilaration to your life.

Risking is the strength you use to do something in spite of the risk of losing or being hurt. It gives you the strength to risk making a mistake and being wrong.

It gives you the courage to depend upon yourself. It also gives you the courage to depend on other people. Risking is basically an **act of dependence**. Through this strength you "cast your bread upon the waters."

Through your risking strength you <u>experience</u> life.

Both thinking and risking are happening in your life all the time. However, they do so unevenly. Sometimes your thinking is most active. At other times, the reverse is true; your risking strength has the major role.

As I sit at the computer writing this book, the focus is on my thinking. I am thinking more than I am risking. This does not mean that my risking strength is inactive. On the contrary, I am still using my risking strength, but it is in a subordinate role. When I present these ideas to a seminar audience, I call mostly on my risking strength. I run the risk of making mistakes, being misunderstood, rejected, put down or ignored.

Here are two real life stories about how each of these two strengths saved my life. They happened when I was a Naval Aviator during World War II.

The first story is about my experience during

a training exercise. I was a Patrol Plane Commander and as such, had my own plane and a crew of four people.

We were preparing for duty in the Pacific. Our mission was to "kill" Japanese submarines. We did it by dropping depth charges that exploded under water near the submarine.

Our training gave us practice in dropping the depth charges on a target "sub." In practice, we used dummy depth charges and dropped them near a U. S. submarine.

This exercise happened at night. The target submarine was cruising in the Pacific Ocean about 25 miles off the coast of San Francisco. It was pitch dark. We were headed due west, going towards the target area.

We were going away from the lights of San Francisco into blackness. This called for flying on instruments. Now, I had been trained in instrument flying as a Cadet, but had very little actual experience doing it. My flying experience had been as a flight instructor in primary flight.

After receiving my "wings" I was assigned as a Primary Flight Instructor. In primary flight we flew a two-wing, open cockpit airplane. All the flying was visual and "seat-of-the-pants."

In doing this type of flying I developed a strong intuitive "feel" for the plane while it was in flight. This feel gave me skill in flying the plane visually. On the other hand, the competence I had developed in instrument flying withered away through the lack of use.

As we flew towards the target "sub," I automatically went on instruments. My instruments indicated that I was flying straight and level. For some reason I developed a "sense" that the plane was banking to the left. My feel told me that the plane was turning.

On the other hand, my instruments showed that the plane was flying straight and level. My feel was telling me one thing and my instruments were telling me another. Which was I to follow, my strong feel or the instruments?

I instinctively followed my feel and lowered my right wing to put the plane in a level position. However, when I did this, the instruments indicated that I was turning to the right. Now I was confused.

In my confusion I kept going back and forth – from feel to instruments – from instruments to feel. Finally, I made the choice to go with the instruments and against my feel.

This was not easy for me to do! It was a gut-wrenching decision to let go of my dependence on my strong feel. It had served me so well in the past. But something gave me the good sense to do it.

With full attention on the instruments, my intuitive feel faded away. My lost skill in instrument flying started coming back. We arrived at the target area on time and went through the exercises. Then, we returned to base safely.

Flying by instruments saved us from crashing into the ocean. In the next story, flying the plane by the seat of my pants probably saved my life.

This second story begins at a Naval Air Station in Oklahoma. We were based there while modifying our planes for duty overseas.

My crew was ordered to fly one of our planes to Philadelphia Naval Air Station. Our Skipper needed to go to Des Moines, Iowa so he signed on as a passenger. We took off with Des Moines as our first stop. This first leg was uneventful. We refueled in Des Moines and took off for Philadelphia.

A few miles west of Joliet, Illinois the right engine suddenly quit. I feathered the prop and gave full power to the other engine. I wanted to see if we could maintain our altitude.

In the event we were unable to hold our altitude we would have to crash land the plane. So I gave the order for all crewmembers and passengers to put on their parachutes.

Fortunately, we were able to maintain our altitude. So we settled down a bit. Since things seemed to be under control, I decided to see if we could restart the failed engine.

My Plane Captain was well acquainted with the fuel system. So I asked him to come forward and work with me in trying to restart the engine. While we were doing this the other engine quit.

All of a sudden we had **no** engines! Wow!

My heart skipped a beat then pounded away. I was excited and scared. I went on "automatic" flying the plane.

This plane had a very high wing loading and without power dropped like a rock. It also had a real bad reputation for leaving no survivors in a crash landing. I gave the order to abandon plane.

I had neglected to put on my own chute. So all I could do was to stay in my seat and do the best I could to bring the plane down in a crash landing. We were flying at an altitude of only 2500 feet. The plane was going down rapidly. So I didn't have much maneuvering room. About all I could do was to land straight ahead, hoping for a clear and level field to land on.

As luck would have it, I was headed for an open cornfield. The field was on the far side of a road running perpendicular to my line of flight. The bad thing was that there were large ditches on both sides of the road. If I was unable to make it over the ditches it would probably wipe out the plane – and me along with it!

On the other hand, if I could get over the ditches I could probably land the plane in the cornfield. If I could set the plane down in a tail-low landing perhaps it would just slide to a stop. The landing wheels were still in an "up" position.

Here is where my ability to fly the plane by feel probably saved my life. For two years I had trained students to land tail first at stall speed. This experience had enabled me to develop skill in landing a plane at its' slowest speed.

Fortune was with me! I was able to clear the ditches and land in the cornfield. As the plane skidded along the field I watched the right engine tear off and go under the wing. This turned the plane at an angle as we skidded to a stop in a cloud of dust.

I had opened the escape hatch above the pilot's seat as the plane was coming down. I did this so I could get out as soon as possible. I was sure it would burn immediately on impact. I was thrown against the instrument panel at first impact and received a small cut above my left eye. But I was still in full control of my faculties.

When the plane came to a rest I climbed through the escape hatch and scrambled down the wing to the ground. I wanted to know if there was anyone left in the plane. So I went through the opening where the cabin door used to be and took a look. None were there – all had jumped!

I can't help but tell you about the old farmer who came up to me at about this time. He held out a bottle of whiskey and said "Here Son, you need a drink." I said, "I sure do" and took a good swig – boy, was I shaking!

By this time the plane was burning at the engine mounts where the engines had torn off. People had started to gather. Some of them were unloading the cargo to save it from the fire. I was yelling to them to stop and get away from the plane. I thought it would explode any minute. Fortunately, the Highway Patrol arrived at about this time and was able to clear the people away before the plane exploded. And explode it did, then burned to the ground.

The saddest part of all was the death of my co-pilot. He had jumped with his chute on but it had not opened before he hit the ground. It was speculated that perhaps he was too low when he jumped and there wasn't enough time for his chute to open (he was the last one to leave the plane). The other possibility was that he couldn't find the rip cord handle in time. He had put his chute on upside down.

A Board of Investigation was assembled. The wreckage was inspected. All crewmembers and passengers were questioned. The final ruling of the board was that the cause was "100% undetermined."

I don't know to this day what caused the engines to fail. I still wonder if the modifications in the fuel system had something to do with it. There was not enough evidence in the burned wreckage to answer this question. There was some talk of sabotage at the Des Moines Airport where we refueled. But as far as I know there was no good evidence of that.

So we have two stories. My thinking and my risking strengths were active in both. However, one or the other was always dominant.

In the first story my ability to fly by instruments saved

us from a crashing into the ocean. *Thinking* is the primary strength used in instrument flying.

In the second story the reverse was true. My intuitive feel for flying the plane enabled me to crash land the plane at its' slowest speed. This probably saved my life. *Risking* is the primary strength used to develop a feel for flying a plane.

I am grateful for both my *thinking* strength and my *risking* strength. In all likelihood, each one, in its' turn, saved my life.

The Thinking Pair
Practical Thinking and Theoretical Thinking

Your practical thinking lets you know what ***has happened*** in the past. It is a fact-oriented strength. It is your common sense. Within this strength lies your capacity to perceive reality – the way things really are!

On the other side, your theoretical thinking lets you know what could happen in the future. It is an idea-oriented strength. It enables you to see the possibilities. With it you create a vision. You use it to set your goals. You imagine how things could be!

The scientific method places an emphasis on these two thinking strengths. Let's follow Newton's thinking as he discovered the Law of Gravity:

As Newton sat under the apple tree, an apple

fell on his head (so the story goes). In thinking about this event he had an idea. The idea was that there was a force pulling all things towards the earth. He went from a specific event to a general principle. *This is an example of theoretical thinking.*

The next thing Newton needed to do was to conduct a controlled experiment. So he dropped all sorts of things to see if indeed they did fall when they weren't supported. He tested his idea against reality. Here, he went from a general principle to specific events. He wanted to see if his idea would work in the real world. *This is an example of practical thinking.*

Newton's use of both types of thinking is a good example of the Scientific Method. It also illustrates the nature of *creative thinking*.

You may have picked up some new ideas in this book. This is your theoretical thinking operating. If so, it is likely that you have been thinking about their practical use. This is your practical thinking. In doing both you are engaged in *creative thinking*!

Einstein was a gifted theoretical thinker. He was also a gifted practical thinker. He used both types of thinking in doing his work.

The Risking Pair
In-dependent Risking
and
Out-dependent Risking

Your risking strength gives you the courage to depend upon a source of strength in spite of the risk of it letting you down.

You risk dependence in two ways. You depend upon your own strengths *and* you depend upon the strengths of other people. Both are "acts of courage." It takes just as much courage to do one as it does to do the other.

Let's first consider in-dependent risking . . .

When you express in-dependent risking, you are placing your trust in yourself. When I started my own consulting business I was using my in-dependent risking. I had very little money and no outside source of income. I had a family to support. Some people regarded my action as foolhardy. But I had confidence in my ability to obtain clients and do the work well. This self-confidence gave me the courage to risk going out on my own.

You express your in-dependent risking by doing your own thinking; following your own convictions; standing-up for what you feel is right; and honestly expressing your real thoughts and feelings.

When you rely on your own strengths, you have both successes and failures. When you have successes, you become aware of your real strengths. When you have failures, you become aware of your limitations. It takes both painful failures and satisfying successes to make you aware of who you really are. This awareness is what gives you self-confidence.

You gain prestige and power by being independent. You keep it by expressing out-dependence.

Now, let's consider out-dependent risking.

Out-dependent risking is the strength you use when you depend on others – trust them. You let your weight down on them and rely upon them to support you.

When expressing out-dependent risking, you focus your attention on others – you become involved with them. You value them. You are concerned for their well-being and show them respect. You think about them and *their* problems. You put yourself in their shoes and try to understand where they are coming from.

When you depend on other people, you run the risk of their taking advantage of you – hurting you and letting you down. You never know for sure until you actually trust them and see what happens. It is always a risk and it takes courage to do it.

When you depend upon others they tend to give you their support and approval. In this way you gather strength from them. You feel more secure and confident. By risking dependence on others you build a solid base of support. This base of support gives you courage to risk independence.

This completes our discussion on the three pairs of strengths that make up your self. Now we are ready to discuss how these core strengths are put together within you.

Your Pattern of Core Strengths

Wherever we find paired opposites, we always find that one is dominant. We find this in brain dominance, also in left and right-handedness. This principle holds true in the three pairs of core strengths.

We refer to the stronger strength in each pair as a *lead strength*. The lesser strength is referred to as a *supporting strength*.

Having lead and supporting strengths makes you *out-of-balance* in the core of your being. Your lop-sided nature makes you a real person – an authentic Human Being. It causes problems for you and other people. That's fine – it's the human condition.

On the positive side, it is where your *consciousness* is born. Having and solving problems is what creates your consciousness. Your conscious awareness gives you the capacity to understand and experience life in its' fullness.

Your core strengths produce personality traits. The charts on pages 28 through 33 describe these traits.

Here's how to use these charts. First, identify your three lead strengths. Then, read all the material under each of your lead strengths. The section, *Natural Way of Being*, describes how you think and behave when you are being yourself. The *Flexibility* section describes how you change when you emphasize your supporting strength in that pair.

Personality Characteristics Produced by Each of the Six Core Strengths

Thinking

NATURAL WAY OF BEING

If **thinking** is your lead strength, you are, by nature, a stable person—more oriented toward thought than action. You think things through and reason things out. Rationality and logic guide your behavior. You analyze situations and develop a well-thought-out plan before taking action.

You tend to be emotionally reserved. You hold your feelings within rather than express them. You are somewhat cautious in establishing new relationships and usually wait for the other person to take the initiative. You like some formality in your relationships. You prefer a relationship that is stable, long-lasting and comfortable.

FLEXIBILITY

When you emphasize your supporting strength in **risking**, you become much more dynamic and active. You express your thoughts and feelings more openly. You take more initiative in your relationships. You move into action more quickly and with more vigor and force. You take more chances and expose yourself more to the risk of failure. Your reactions become more spontaneous and free. You seek to have more influence on others. You generate more excitement and enthusiasm.

Risking

NATURAL WAY OF BEING

If risking is your lead strength, you are, by nature, a dynamic person—more oriented toward action than thought. You are a doer. You get involved and express your thoughts and feelings. You tend to decide quickly and move into action without much delay. You trust your feelings and make your decisions on intuitive feel.

You enjoy dynamic interactions with other people. You take the initiative in your relationships and you expect others to respond to you with vigor. You seek to have a strong influence on other people. You generate excitement and enthusiasm. You want to be active doing something and you prefer doing it with other people.

FLEXIBILITY

When you emphasize your supporting strength in thinking, you become more thoughful and reflective. You slow yourself down and take more time to make your decisions. You do more planning and do a better job in anticipating future problems. You are more reserved in your relationships. You give the other person time to respond. You back off and don't come on so strong.

Practical Thinking

NATURAL WAY OF BEING

If **practical thinking** is your lead strength, you are, by nature, a practical, fact-oriented person. You see things as they are and accept the realities of a situation. You tend to be conservative and base your decisions on solid facts. You are problem-centered and solve your problems in a step-by-step, orderly fashion. You are likely to have a good deal of common sense.

You are a down-to-earth person who likes to deal with today's problems rather than tomorrow's possibilities. You prefer to deal with factual and specific information rather than generalities. You are more interested in applying ideas than you are in the ideas themselves. You keep your feet on the ground and take a pragmatic approach. You are a realistic person who looks straight at the facts.

FLEXIBILITY

When you emphasize your supporting strength in **theoretical thinking,** you show more interest in theory and abstract ideas. You become more reflective and philosophical. You ask the question "Why?" more frequently and are more interested in discovering the general principle. You become more open to new ideas and you look more toward the future. When you emphasize your theoretical thinking, you become more imaginative and flexible in finding solutions to problems.

Theoretical Thinking

NATURAL WAY OF BEING

If **theoretical thinking** is your lead strength, you are, by nature, an idea-oriented person. You have a natural ability to understand abstract concepts. You seek to identify general principles and look for connections between isolated events. You enjoy becoming aware of general laws and theories that explain why things are the way they are. You tend to synthesize information rather than analyze it. You appreciate ideas for their own sake. You are a global thinker. You tend to speculate about possibilities and look for alternate solutions. You are flexible in your thinking and can usually appreciate different points of view. You may have an active imagination. You are idealistic. You tend to see how things could be more clearly than you see how things really are. You like to study philosophy and speculate about fundamental truths.

FLEXIBILITY

When you emphasize your supporting strength in **practical thinking,** you become more realistic and fact-oriented. You become more practical and develop skill in using your ideas to solve practical problems. You more readily accept reality and develop effectiveness in dealing with immediate practical situations. You show more common sense and practical judgment in dealing with the real world

Out-Dependent Risking

NATURAL WAY OF BEING

If **out-dependent risking** is your lead strength, you are likely to enjoy working with a group. You tend to be co-operative and have a ready willingness to consider the views of others. You get along well with others. You are a good listener and are easy to talk to.

Relationships with others are very important to you. You have a natural tendency to share with others and develop the strength of a group. You are inclined to delegate and draw on the strengths of others. You seek other people's opinions and rely on what they have to say. Their support and approval are very important to you.

You are people-oriented and experience a good deal of warmth toward others. You are accepting, understanding, and tolerant of other people. You are supportive in your relationships and others tend to feel comfortable with you. You are a caring person who is naturally helpful—it is part of your basic nature.

FLEXIBILITY

When you emphasize your supporting strength in **In-dependent risking,** you become more self-reliant, self-directed and self-confident. You assume more personal responsibility and rely more on your own strengths to solve your problems. You develop more self-respect and feelings of self-worth. Your increased self-esteem enables you to relate to others on a more objective basis and with a stronger sense of equality. When you emphasize your in-dependent strengths, you display more leadership qualities and experience more self-confidence.

In-Dependent Risking

NATURAL WAY OF BEING

If **In-dependent risking** is your lead strength, by nature, you tend to be self-sufficient and have a good deal of self-confidence. You think things through on your own and follow your own convictions. You depend on your self more than you depend on others. You stand on your own two feet and make your own decisions. You tend to keep your own counsel and work things through on your own.

You are ambitious and goal-oriented. You select your own goals and take the initiative to accomplish them. You are anxious to accomplish your goals and experience a good deal of impatience with any delays. You want to be somebody and make your mark.

You gravitate toward a leadership role. You tend to feel a good deal of personal responsibility in anything that you do. You value your independence and personal freedom. You are stimulated by a challenge and have a strong desire to win. You tend to be competitive with others. You are territorial and have a ready willingness to fight for what you consider to be your rights.

FLEXIBILITY

When you emphasize your supporting strength in **out-dependent risking,** you become a warmer and more accepting person. You pay more attention to other people and draw more heavily on their strengths. You become more understanding and supportive of the other person. You listen more carefully to others and try to understand their points of view. You develop more patience and build stronger ties with other people. You become a more caring person and participate more fully in the strength of the group.

Eight Patterns of Core Strength

You have a lead strength in each of the three pairs. Your ***Pattern of Core Strengths*** *is determined by which are your three lead strength.*

There are eight different combinations of three *lead* strengths. Each combination is assigned a pattern number. These eight combinations and their pattern number are listed on the next page.

The combination in which *all three* are your lead strengths is referred to as your "Core Pattern." The three combinations in which you have *two* lead strengths are your three "Flex-Patterns." The three combinations in which you have *one* lead strength are your three "Distant Patterns." The combination in which you have *no* lead strength is your "Opposite Pattern."

Three Lead Strengths Pattern Number

Thinking	Prac. Think.	Out-dep. Risk.	I
Thinking	Prac. Think.	In-dep. Risk.	II
Thinking	Theo. Think.	Out-dep. Risk.	III
Thinking	Theo. Think.	In-dep. Risk.	IV
Risking	Prac. Think.	Out-dep. Risk.	V
Risking	Theo. Think	Out-dep. Risk.	VI
Risking	Prac. Think.	In-dep. Risk	VII
Risking	Theo. Think.	In-dep. Risk.	VIII

Suggestion: Underline your three *lead* strengths each time they appear in the chart. This makes it easy for you to identify your "core pattern," three "flex-patterns," three "distant patterns" and "opposite pattern."

The chart, *Eight Patterns of Core Strengths*, on pages 38 and 39 decribes the personality traits produced by each pattern. Here are suggestions on how to use the chart:

> First, identify your core pattern and your three flex-patterns.
>
> Second, underline the words in these four patterns that you feel describe you.
>
> Third, count the words you have underlined in each of these four patterns.
>
> If you find that you have underlined more words in one of your flex-patterns than in your core pattern, it may be your real core pattern.
>
> You may find it instructive to read the words in your opposite pattern. Sometimes this confirms your core pattern by describing who you are *not*.

The "worth" or "value" of these patterns needs discussion:

You need to value the worth of the patterns from two perspectives.

One perspective is to value them in terms of their contributions to limited projects in the world. From this view, some patterns contribute more to certain projects than do others. Your pattern equips you to do some jobs better than others. From this perspective the patterns have *unequal* value.

The other view is to look at the patterns as they fit into the creation process as a whole. Here, we have no basis on which to judge their value. We don't know what the whole is. So all we can say is that one pattern is just as "worthy" as any other pattern – no better and no worse. The patterns have equal value from this perspective. You have every right to feel good about your pattern whatever it may be.

Eight Patterns

I STRENGTHS

LEAD **supporting**

THINKING / risking
PRACTICAL / theoretical
OUT-DEPENDENT / in-dependent

Stable, dependable, steady, orderly, quiet, consistent,methodical, cautious, receptive, hesitant, accepting, respecfful, conforming, attentive, economical, practical systematic, loyal.

Good listener—Maintains stability
Leads change carefully

II STRENGTHS

LEAD **supporting**

THINKING / risking
PRACTICAL / theoretical
IN-DEPENDENT / out-dependent

Rational, logical, analytical, objective, firm, deliberate, self-reliant, strong-willed, calm, conservative, industrious, self-controlled, determined, prudent, discerning, realistic, tenacious, disciplined.

Fact oriented — Uses common sense
Leads change in an orderly way

III STRENGTHS

LEAD **supporting**

THINKING / risking
THEORETICAL / practical
OUT-DEPENDENT / in-dependent

Thoughtful, polite, sincere, knowledgeable, learned, academic, scholarly, sensitive, shy, mild-mannered, gentle, faithful, dutiful, patient, tolerant, benevolent, studious, courteous.

Explains concepts — Nurtures others
Leads researched change

IV STRENGTHS

LEAD **supporting**

THINKING / risking
THEORETICAL / practical
IN-DEPENDENT / out-dependent

Contemplative, reflective, introspective, philosophical, insighfful, precise, accurate, experimental, serious, intense, persistent, self-sufficient, profound, earnest. inventive, individualistic, perceptive, ingenious.

Intuitive thinker — Creates new concepts
Leads conceptual change

# of Core Strengths

V STRENGTHS

LEAD supporting

RISKING / thinking
PRACTICAL / theoretical
OUT-DEPENDENT / in-dependent

Outgoing, friendly, sociable, cordial, caring, talkative, generous, adaptable, supportive, giving, helpful, flexible, gregarious, likable cooperative, accommodating, big-hearted, sympathetic.

Coordinator — People oriented
Leads cooperative change

VI STRENGTHS

LEAD supporting

RISKING / thinking
THEORETICAL / practical
OUT-DEPENDENT / in-dependent

Diplomatic, gracious, hospitable, trusting, open, responsive, compassionate, liberal, empathetic, hopeful, humorous, cheerful, soft-hearted, demonstrative, idealistic, artful, affectionate, expressive.

Socially adept — Warm relator
Leads change with sensitivity to others

VII STRENGTHS

LEAD supporting

RISKING / thinking
PRACTICAL / theoretical
IN-DEPENDENT / out-dependent

Self-assertive, decisive, resourceful, active, action-oriented, enterprising, self-confident, goal-oriented, vigorous, energetic, forceful, ambitious, doer, adventurous, self-starting, competitive, outspoken, takes initiative.

Drives hard to achieve goals
Leads change in a forcetul way

VIII STRENGTHS

LEAD supporting

RISKING / thinking
THEORETICAL / practical
IN-DEPENDENT / out-dependent

Dynamic, spirited, convincing, optimistic, dramatic, impulsive, imaginative, colorful, eloquent, innovative, versatile, exciting, charismatic, inspirational, enthusiastic, persuasive, impelling, exuberant.

Promotes Ideas — Out-front leader
Leads dramatic change

Thomas Inventory of Core Strengths

The most accurate way to identify your pattern is to complete the *Thomas Inventory of Core Strengths.*

This *Inventory* is scientifically validated. It has been in use for over 25 years. Until recently it has been made available only to Professionals. A special version of the instrument is now available to the general public through our website.

The *Thomas Inventory of Core Strengths* is actually a packet of six *Inventories*. One you fill out on yourself. The other five are filled out on you by people you select. The data gathered from all six forms are computer analyzed and the results are given to you on a Computer Report Form.

The Report Form that you receive shows your Core Pattern, three Flex-Patterns, three Distant Patterns and Opposite Pattern. In addition, the Report Form reveals how each of the five other people see you.

For up-to-date information about the online version of the *Thomas Inventory of Core Strengths*, please visit our website at

http.//www.inpsyte.com

Innate Capacities of the Natural Self

Our "selves" are the same in that we all have the same six Core Strengths. Our "selves" are different, however, in two important ways. One difference is that we have different *Patterns of Core Strengths.* The other difference is in our *Innate Capacities.*

Your pattern and your innate capacities are distinctly different. Your pattern is strictly an internal matter. It is how your own strengths relate to one another. On the other hand, your innate capacities are measures of *how much* strength you have compared to other people.

> *Your pattern is the internal arrangement of your own strengths – how you are wired up. Your innate capacity is* ***how much*** *strength you have compared to others.*

Basic mental abilities and energy potential are good examples of innate capacities.

Your innate capacities are an important part of your natural self. However, they haven't been the focus of our attention. As a result, our approach has little to offer beyond affirming their importance. Innate Capacities comprise one of the Four Life Forces that play a role in forming your personality. These Four Life Forces are discussed in detail in chapter 2, *Your Personality.*

We have the same value system in regard to innate capacities as in the Patterns. There are vast differences in how much we can contribute to limited projects in the world. We are *unequal* in this regard.

The other view is to see our innate capacities as a part of the creation process as a whole. From this viewpoint we have no basis to value capacities – we don't know what the whole is. So all we can say is that we are *equally* valuable to the total. This is true regardless of how much capacity we may have.

Chapter 2

Your Personality

How does my personality differ from my natural self? How is my personality formed? What forces create it? Does my personality change or remain the same? If I can change it, how do I go about it? These are the types of questions addressed in this chapter.

Your natural self comes into being at the time of your conception. The genetic structures that determine it were set when you were conceived. They remain constant throughout your lifetime.

On the other hand, your *personality* is a changing thing. It is shaped by your reactions to your environment. Your reactions are both conscious and unconscious.

Your *unconscious* reactions begin at the time you are conceived in the womb. They continue until you die. Your *conscious* reactions come at a later time. They begin when your awareness reaches a certain point.

This point is described in various ways. Some say it is the time when you know the difference between right and wrong. Others say it comes with your "dawn of consciousness." Still others define it as the point where you develop a "conscience."

We define it as the point where you have the power to make conscious personal choices. These are choices you make in what you pay attention to and how you behave.

Thomas Theory of Personality

Your personality is created by four *Life Forces*. These forces are:

(1) Pattern of Core Strengths
[Your combination of lead and supporting Strengths]

(2) Innate Capacities
[**How much** strength you have compared to other people]

(3) Environment
[**Outside forces** that influence how you express your natural self in the world]

(4) Personal Choices
[The conscious choices you make in directing your attention and controlling your behavior]

These Four Forces are described in more detail in the chart titled THOMAS THEORY OF PERSONALITY on the next page (45).

Thomas Theory of Personality

Two forces create the natural self

1. **PATTERN OF CORE STRENGTHS**
   Pure strengths – no weaknesses
   Inborn tendencies
   Basic inclinations
   Natural creativeness
2. **INNATE CAPACITIES**
   Mental abilities – intelligence
   Drive – energy potential
   Individual talents
   Aptitudes

Two forces influence how the natural self is expressed in the world.

3. **ENVIRONMENT**
   Primarily other people
   Education and training
   Society and culture
   Value systems – attitudes
4. **PERSONAL CHOICES**
   Conscious awareness
   Freedom of choice – free will
   Choosing what we pay attention to
   Choosing how we behave

These Four Forces Have Equal Potential To Shape The Personality.

The influence of each of the forces varies. Sometimes environment has the most influence. At other times personal choice has the greater influence. At still other times *your natural self* plays the major role.

The First Two Forces

The first two forces are your pattern of core strengths and your innate capacities. They create your natural self. They are the enduring forces that stay the same throughout your lifetime. They are genetically determined.

Your *natural self* is positive and good. Although it is out-of-balance and limited, there is nothing bad or evil about it. Its' nature is to grow and progress. All you need to do is to accept it and faithfully express it in your daily living. There is certainly no reason for you to wish it were different or try to change it.

There are no favored "selves" – some better or more desirable than others. Each natural self is a unique creation. Each has its' own niche to fill in the Creation Process.

Many have an opposite view. This view is that there is something wrong or bad about the natural self. This view leads to the notion that the natural self needs to be controlled or made over in some way. There are at least three things wrong with this view:

First, it is very destructive to the growth and development of the individual.

Second, it inhibits the growth and progress of Human society.

Third, it causes us to waste energy in trying to change something that we cannot change.

There is plenty of bad and evil in the world. But it doesn't come from the natural self. It comes from the bad personal choices made by people. In turn, these bad choices create a bad environment. This brings us to the second two life forces.

The Second Two Forces

The second two forces – Environment and Personal Choices – provide for your growth and development. Through these two forces you can change your personality.

Here's an illustration:

> One of our most effective Seminar Leaders has Pattern I Strengths. His natural way is to be practical, thoughtful, quiet, accepting and focused on other people.
>
> When he leads a seminar he behaves in a different way. In this leadership situation he changes. He takes initiative, talks a lot and displays a good deal of self-confidence.
>
> His personality changes but his core pattern remains the same. His Pattern I strengths are still in the background, flavoring everything he does.

Here's another illustration:

A client with whom I worked for years was a natural Pattern VII. During one of our conversations we were comparing him with his cousin. His cousin was a natural Pattern II. My client said to me, "Jay, I can be a Pattern II, but when I am, I'm a Pattern II like a VII is." This may be a clumsy way to say it, but it certainly gets at the thought I am trying to convey.

You can change your personality through Personal Choice. But when you do your natural self still shows through.

It is through environment and personal choice that the negative and destructive enter the picture. You can have either a good or bad environment. The same is true of personal choices. You can make either good or bad personal choices.

Environment

Your environment is an outside influence. People are the primary source of these influences. How your parents relate to you makes a big difference. Their attitudes play an important role in determining your own attitudes. Your education and training have an influence. The society in which you live have an impact. You tend to take on the values of your culture.

Here's a personal example:

> I grew up in a culture that placed a high value on independence. Conversely, dependence was regarded as a weakness.
>
> I took on this value system. I am sure I didn't figure it out on my own. My environment laid it on me.
>
> It was hard for me to admit that I was dependent on others. I thought it was a sign of weakness. My goal was to become independently wealthy. Then, I wouldn't have to be dependent on anybody.
>
> I no longer think this way. Now I see dependence on others as strength. This doesn't mean that the value system laid on me by my early environment has completely gone away. The scar of my early learning is still there and probably always will be. But it fades as time goes by.

In this story my environment was a bad influence. It taught me a wrong value system. I hasten to add, however, that my environment also taught me many good things, as well. I am grateful to my parents for teaching me the value of honesty and hard work.

You have **no** control over your past environment. It is a fact and will remain a fact forever. Also, you have no control over your present environment. It is already here. All you can do is respond to it.

However, you do have **some** control over your future environment. You can make a personal choice to get out of a hurtful environment. Sometimes these are painful and difficult choices. But if you make the hard choice you can usually find a way to make the change.

A bad environment is not always hurtful to us. We can turn a bad environment into a good learning experience.

Here is an example:

> The first thing I do in working with a client is to have an evaluation interview. During this interview I ask the question, "Who has had the greatest influence in your life?"
>
> On one occasion a young engineer responded by saying, "Well, I guess it was my Dad. He was an alcoholic and a shiftless bum. My Mother took care of us kids and I had little to do with my Dad. He showed me what not to do with my life."

This kind of response happened more than once. Others with whom I have counseled responded in a similar way. You **can** use a bad environment to your advantage. You can, through Personal Choice, make lemonade out of lemons.

Personal Choices

It is natural for you to grow and mature up to the point of your "*dawn of consciousness.*" Your conscious awareness gives you the freedom to choose. The power to make Personal Choices. This power, in so far as we know, has been given only to Human Beings.

You don't choose this freedom; the Creation Process thrusts it upon you.

Gaining the power of Personal Choice is a pivotal point in your growth. No longer is your growth simply natural and automatic. **Now, you must consciously choose to be a part of the growth process.**

This gift of freedom to choose is a good thing. It allows you to live life on a conscious level. You experience more deeply all the joys of being alive.

You are accountable for how you use this freedom. It is a forced choice situation. You choose to be a part of the Creation Process or, in failing to do so, lose your rightful place in it. You lose by default!

If you make choices in harmony with the creative process, you grow. You gain more freedom. You develop more inner strength and become more productive.

If you fail to make these positive choices you distort the expression of creative strength. You lose your freedom. You suffer increasing pain and frustration. This pain is your signal to make a positive choice.

Your freedom of choice is what gives you the power to control your life. Here's a story told to me by a client. He relates how he used his power of personal choice to quit smoking.

> I started smoking when very young, probably around twelve. I had been smoking for over 35 years. I had tried to quit numerous times through the years, but had always gone back to smoking again. I was a real expert at "quitting smoking!"

About five years ago I was having frequent headaches. I connected these headaches with my smoking. This motivated me even more to stop. Now I really did want to quit smoking for good.

Why did I start smoking again when I really didn't want to? As I thought about it, it dawned on me that every time I started to smoke again, I was thinking about it. When I dwelled on the thought of smoking I developed a powerful urge to smoke. I developed a lot of will power – "I **will** smoke," and invariably did.

With this insight I developed a plan. The plan was real simple. I would deliberately shift my thinking to something else when I caught myself thinking about smoking.

Here's how I put my plan to work:

I was sitting at my desk doing paper work and caught myself starting to think about smoking. I willfully turned my attention to the work I needed to do. I became busily engaged in doing the work.

It wasn't long before the thought of smoking returned. Keeping with my plan, I shifted my thoughts back to my work again and concentrated on the task.

The thought of smoking continued to reoccur. But it became more and more infrequent. As time went along, it seemed to get easier for me to make the shift back to my work.

I made it through the day without smoking.

When I went home that evening I continued the plan. Each time the thought of smoking came to my mind I shifted my thinking to something else. After making the shift in my thinking, I got busy doing what I was thinking about.

I continued to practice my new discipline the next day at work. As the day progressed the thought of smoking came to me less and less. At the end of the day I suddenly realized that I hadn't thought of smoking for the past couple of hours!

It was downhill after that. It has been five years since I have smoked. Now I don't even think about it unless someone else brings it up. When this happens, I just shift my thinking to something else and the urge to smoke never appears.

Chapter 3

Being Yourself

The next three chapters focus on your power of personal choice. There are three choices you must make to be psychologically healthy. Your first choice is to *be yourself*. This choice is discussed in this chapter. We deal with the other two – *being flexible* and *avoiding polarization* – in the next two chapters.

Your first healthy step into life is being yourself. Being who you were created to be – being your natural self.

When you were a child the admonition to "be yourself" had no meaning. You didn't have the power to choose otherwise. When you became self-conscious, being yourself became a matter of choice. Now you must *choose* to *be yourself*. In failing to do so, you become either a phony or a nobody.

Here are some ways to describe what you are doing when you are being yourself:

You are . . . .
. . . . expressing your Pattern of Core Strengths
. . . . using all of your Innate Capacities
. . . . doing what comes naturally
. . . . being true to yourself
. . . . doing it your way
. . . . filling your niche

.... being a real and authentic person
.... expressing your Natural Tendencies

Natural Tendencies

A natural tendency is an inborn inclination to favor your lead strengths.

For example:

If you favor **Thinking,** you tend to be quiet and listen when it's time to speak out.

If you favor **Risking,** you tend to talk when it's time to listen.

If you favor **Practical Thinking,** you tend to dwell on the past when it's time to look to the future.

If you favor **Theoretical Thinking,** you tend to think of possibilities when it's time to look at the facts.

If you favor **In-dependent Risking,** you tend to do things yourself when it's time to rely on others.

If you favor **Out-dependent Risking,** you tend to depend on others when it's time to be more independent.

When you express a natural tendency you create problems, both for yourself and others. Does this mean that a natural tendency is bad and you ought to get rid of it? We give a resounding "no" answer to this question.

Natural tendencies are not bad, nor should you try to get rid of them. As a healthy Human Being you need to go ahead and express your natural tendencies. You do it in spite of the problems they may cause. The larger value is that you are faithful in playing your assigned role in the Creation Process.

Listed below are thirty-one common tendencies. In reading the list most people find that they express a number of them.

TENDENCY TO . . . .

1. talk when it's time to listen.

2. avoid confrontation and conflict when it's time to express your own thoughts and feelings

3. withdraw into own self-sufficiency when it's time to draw on the strengths of others.

4. imagine the possibilities when it's time to get the facts.

5. say "yes" when it's time to say "no."

6. wait for the other person to make the first move when it's time for you to take the initiative.

7. compete with others when it's time to be more cooperative.

8. hold onto established ways when it's time to try something new.

9. keep emotionally involved when it's time to be more objective.

10. go along with others when itís time to go your own way.

11. keep going over the problem when it's time to look for solutions.

12. make the decision when it's time to do more thinking.

13. hold feeling inside when it's time to express them.

14. keep focused on your own goals when it's time to consider the goals of others.

15. look for the general principle when it's time to solve a practical problem.

16. depend on others when it's time to be more independent.

17. do things yourself when it's time to rely on others,

18. be sympathetic and supportive when it's time to require others to be more responsible.

19. change things when it's time to keep things the way they are.

20. dwell on the past when it's time to look to the future.

21. be impatient when it's time to be more understanding.

22. do things that pleases others when it's time to pay more attention to your own needs.

23. be quiet and listen when it's time to speak out.

24. take risks when it's time to be more conservative.

25. speculate about possibilities when it's time to deal with a practical problem.

26. think own thoughts when it's time to pay attention to what others are saying.

27. analyze the problem when it's time to take action.

28. express own thoughts and feelings when it's time to be more reserved and quiet.

29. be tolerant of others when it's time to be more firm.

30. keep thinking of the present situation when it's time to develop a vision for the future.

31. perfect the plan when it's time to act.

There are two important things to remember about natural tendencies:

(1) We all have them. It's a part of being a normal Human Being.
(2) We need to express them. It's a healthy thing to do.

What does it look like when you are failing to be yourself? Here is a story of a woman who came home to herself while attending one of our seminars. She had spent years trying to be what others thought she should be, rather than being her real self.

> Her *Inventory* results showed that her three lead strengths were **Risking, Practical Thinking**, and **In-dependent Risking**. This made her a Pattern VII.
>
> When the *Inventory* results were passed out I noticed that she was shocked and agitated. I made myself available to her so she could talk. She said, "This shows that I am more in-dependent than out-dependent. I certainly don't see myself that way. I don't see how the *Inventories* could show that."
>
> I said, "The *Inventory* results can give us a false reading. However, it's a reliable test. So it's a good idea to pay serious attention to what it is telling us. I suggest that you keep an open mind at this point. You will be getting more information as we go through the rest of the seminar. I would like to talk with you again after the program is over." She accepted my offer. But she was still

confused and upset.

Towards the end of the Seminar she approached me and said, "You know, I think the *Inventories* are right. I do lean more towards independence. All sorts of lights have been coming on for me as we have gone through the program."

"I've been told all my life that I ought to let others do things for me. It wasn't becoming for a woman to show too much independence and self-sufficiency."

"In the past I have considered being dependent and being independent as mutually exclusive – you were either one or the other. Now you are telling me I am both – I have both strengths. You are also saying both are good. That's a new thought for me."

"Now I believe the *Inventories* were right. I am a very independent person. I tried to hide it in the past. In doing so, I tried to be something that wasn't really me. I guess I wasn't doing a very good job of it. Everyone who filled out my *Inventories* saw independence as my lead strength."

"Right now I am feeling better about myself than I have in a long time. It feels really good to just relax and be myself, knowing that it's OK for me to be me."

Now she is ready to come back home to herself. She is free to express her independence. No longer does she need to deny it as she has been doing. This will put her on the road to being a healthier and more real person.

As she expresses her strong independence she will cause problems. But these are healthy problems. She can solve them by being flexible – using her supporting strength in out-dependence. This is how she will develop internal strength.

Habits

Habits are *learned tendencies.* Natural tendencies are a part of your natural self and, as such, are good. On the other hand, habits can be either good or bad.

Recall the story about the man who quit smoking. He didn't have a natural tendency to smoke. He had developed a bad habit of smoking. He broke this bad habit by replacing it with a good habit of doing productive work.

> *Natural tendencies stay the same. Habits can be changed.*

Here's a personal example about me developing a bad habit of going against my natural tendency:

> I have a lead strength in **Thinking** and a supporting strength in **Risking**. I know this about myself for two reasons. First, I feel good and most at home when I am thinking through a problem – more so than when I am risking. Second, my life experiences tell me I am most effective when I am thinking, not when I am risking.
>
> Not long ago I became aware that I was reacting too quickly with people. As a result, I was

making lots of mistakes. Also, I was losing much of my impact. I could have a greater influence on others by giving myself more time to think before responding.

I had formed a bad habit of going against my natural tendency. I was reacting too fast and short-circuiting my thinking strength. What I needed to do was to form a good habit of being myself. I needed to be more deliberate and thoughtful.

Now that I have figured out what is going on I am practicing a more studied response. Three good things are happening. One, I feel more comfortable and confident. Two, I am having a stronger impact. Three, I am more effective in achieving what I want to do.

Using Your Innate Capacities

People differ greatly in their innate capacities.

Some people have more capacity than you do – others have less. Your only obligation is to use the capacity you have, regardless of how you compare with others.

To paraphrase Dwight Eisenhower:

It is not a question of the hand that has been dealt to you, but rather how you play it.

Happiness and a sense of fulfillment come from using what you have, **not** from how much you have compared to others. If you have been given a great deal, there is much you need to do. If you have been given a lesser amount, then all you need to do is to use that which you have been given.

Chapter 4

Being Flexible

In the last chapter we emphasized being yourself. In this chapter we emphasize being flexible. You must do **both** – doing only one is not enough. Each has its' place in living a healthy and productive life.

You may be saying, "Hey, you are talking out of both sides of your mouth. They are opposites. How can I do both?"

The answer is that you do them one at a time. It is like walking. You use the strength in your two legs in an alternating manner. You lead out with one of your legs. It can take you only so far. Then you shift over to the other leg. Again, it takes you only so far. You shift back to the other leg again. This alternating use of your two legs takes you forward.

It is the same with *being yourself* and *being flexible.* You shift your attention back and forth – doing one then the other. In doing both you move forward in growth and progress.

When you are being yourself your focus of attention is *inward.* You become aware of yourself – who you really are. This is how you build your self-confidence.

When you are being flexible your attention is directed outward. You are aware of what's going on outside yourself. This external focus helps you to build good relationships with the world around you.

What are you actually doing when you are being flexible? Here's some ways to say it:

You are . . . .

. . . . emphasizing your supporting strengths.

. . . . solving problems caused by you being yourself.

. . . . paying attention to other people.

. . . . doing what is appropriate to the situation.

. . . . adjusting to your environment.

. . . . "bending with the wind."

. . . . doing what needs to be done.

You stand ready to use any of your six polar strengths. Your focus is on the situation, not yourself.

When you emphasize one of your supporting strengths you express a pattern other than your own core pattern. We refer to these other patterns as your "Flex-patterns."

Flex-Patterns

A flex-pattern is the pattern you express when you emphasize one of your supporting strengths.

Since you have three supporting strengths you have three flex-patterns. You may identify your three flex-patterns on page 68.

The personality characteristics produced by each of your three flex-patterns may be found in the chart, EIGHT PATTERNS OF CORE STRENGTHS on pages 38 and 39.

You will probably find that one of your flex-patterns is easy for you to express – the other two more difficult. In all likelihood, you will discover that one is most difficult. Chances are this is where you need to do most of your work.

When you express a flex-pattern you don't change your core pattern. It remains the same. But you do change your thinking and behavior and this changes your personality.

How does your personality change when you emphasize each of your supporting strengths? These changes are described in the FLEXIBILITY section under each of your lead strengths on pages 28 through 33.

Flex-Patterns

Core pattern	Lead Strengths	Supporting Strengths	Flex-patterns
I	Thinking	Risking	V
	Practical thinking	Theoretical thinking	III
	Out-dependent risking	In-dependent risking	II
II	Thinking	Risking	VII
	Practical thinking	Theoretical thinking	VII
	In-dependent risking	Out-dependent risking	I
III	Thinking	Risking	VI
	Theoretical thinking	Practical thinking	I
	Out-dependent risking	In-dependent risking	IV
IV	Thinking	Risking	VIII
	Theoretical thinking	Practical thinking	IV
	In-dependent risking	Out-dependent risking	III
V	Risking	Thinking	I
	Practical thinking	Theoretical thinking	VI
	Out-dependent risking	In-dependent risking	VII
VI	Risking	Thinking	III
	Theoretical thinking	Practical thinking	V
	Out-dependent risking	In-dependent risking	VII
VII	Risking	Thinking	II
	Practical thinking	Theoretical thinking	VIII
	In-dependent risking	Out-dependent risking	V
VII	Risking	Thinking	IV
	Theoretical thinking	Practical thinking	VII
	In-dependent risking	Out-dependent risking	VI

Here's a story of how an Accountant solved a painful problem by being flexible:

Dave White worked for one of my client companies. He had a high I.Q. – bordering on the genius level. He had graduated with honors from an Ivy League college.

He was respected for his technical competence. Co-workers frequently asked for his advice. He was respectful and people referred to him as a "Nice Guy". He tended to be quiet and reserved in his relationships.

The President of the company asked me to work with Dave. He thought Dave had potential for additional responsibilities. Others talked with me about Dave. There was general agreement that he did have potential. But he wasn't making progress because he didn't assert himself. They thought he needed to be more aggressive.

In my talk with Dave he said, "I have been working for this company for over five years and have made little progress. Oh, I've had a few raises but no real promotion. I'm way behind where I thought I'd be at this time."

"I see problems around here and think I have some solutions. But no one pays much attention to me. Some of the people around here are very pushy and have a loud mouth. They get all the attention. If that's what it takes to get ahead here, then they can count me out. I'm not going to be that way."

He had developed a good deal of hostility towards some of those who were more aggressive.

He continued, "I feel very uncomfortable in our group meetings. It is hard for me to speak up. Others are always jumping in. By the time I have decided what to say the conversation has moved on to something else. A lot of decisions have been made in these meetings that I felt were wrong. But nobody asked me for my opinion. I feel ignored most of the time."

It was apparent that **Thinking** was Dave's lead strength. He regarded thinking as a valuable strength. On the other hand, he saw risking in a negative way. He considered it to be the enemy of sound thinking.

Shortly after my interview with Dave he attended one of our Seminars. He got very involved. It appeared as if he gained insight into his problem.

His Inventories showed that he had Pattern I strengths.

After the seminar I visited with him. He said, "I enjoyed the seminar a lot. I feel a lot better about myself now. I believe I see what has been going on with me. I've just been too quiet. I need to speak up and be more forceful, especially in those group meetings."

"I need to shift into my flex-pattern V and be more assertive. It won't be easy for me because it's not my way. But I can see that I need to do it."

He invited me to sit in on one of their meetings. During the meeting he deliberately forced himself to speak up. At the start, his efforts were tentative and awkward. In spite of this, the group recognized his efforts and gave him their attention.

The group's reaction encouraged him. With practice he became more confident as time went along. His Pattern I strengths still flavored his behavior – he was assertive in a deliberate way. The big change was that now he was much more active in group activities. He acted a lot like a Pattern V.

I met with him after the meeting. He was feeling very good about himself and what had gone on at the meeting. He said, "I felt a lot of anxiety at first. But after awhile I began to feel more comfortable. At the end of the meeting I was feeling very good about it. I intend to be more assertive in my other relationships too." I encouraged him. I also promised to check with him during my next visit to the company.

This story has a happy ending. As a result of his efforts to be more aggressive he became much more productive. His contributions to the company were much greater. After a few months he became the group leader. Along with that he received a healthy raise in salary.

Dave was still being himself. All the good qualities of his natural Pattern 1 strengths were still showing through. The change was that now he was using his supporting strength in risking more fully. He was walking with both legs – being himself and being flexible.

Chapter 5

Avoiding Polarization

Up until now we have been dealing with positives. Our focus has been on how creative strength works in your life. The time has come for us to deal with the negative.

The negative is born of human choice. When we gain the power of Personal Choice we gain the power to garble the expression of creative strength. We don't have the power to create this strength, but we do have the power to distort its' expression.

The intent of this chapter is twofold. First, to help you recognize when you are interfering with the creative process. Second, to help you see what you need to do to stop interfering.

How do we interfere with the creative process? The short answer is that we do it by getting polarized.

Understanding Polarization

Polarization is a two-way street. On the one hand, we over-use one strength in a pair. On the other, we repress the expression of its' opposite strength.

We can polarize on any of our strengths. We tend to polarize on our lead strengths. However, we can, and sometimes do, polarize on our supporting strengths.

What does it look like when you are polarizing on a strength? One way to visualize it is to imagine trying to row a boat by using the oar on only one side. You find yourself going around and around in circles. You are wearing yourself out and not making any headway.

One of our Teachers uses this story:

> A man was sitting beside a pond watching ducks swimming around in the water. He noticed that one duck was having a difficult time keeping up with the others. When it tried to go forward, it would just go around in a circle.
>
> Feeling sorry for the duck, the man picked it up. He discovered that one of its' legs was missing. Being a handyman, he decided to see if he could make an artificial leg for the duck.
>
> He took the duck home. He made an artificial leg with a webfoot. Then he secured it to the stub that was still left. The next day he brought the duck back to the pond and put it in the water. As the duck swam off, straight and true, the man swears that it looked back and gave him a proud grin.

How can you tell when you are polarizing on a particular polar strength? Here are some signs . . . .

Signs of becoming polarized on the Thinking Strength

Continuing to think . . . to think . . . to think
. . . procrastinating
. . . holding feelings inside
. . . resisting change
. . . feeling more and more depressed and "out of it"
. . . finally, becoming immobilized

Signs of becoming polarized on the Risking Strength

Continuing to engage in action . . . engage in action . . . engage in action
. . . making quick decisions
. . . expressing feelings aggressively
. . . resisting thoughtful analysis
. . . feeling increasingly exposed and agitated
. . . finally, being out of control

Signs of becoming polarized on the Practical Thinking Strength

Continuing to think about the problem . . . think about the problem . . . think about the problem
. . . seeing all the rocks in the road
. . . holding onto status quo

. . . using facts as clubs to destroy ideas
. . . feeling pessimistic and gloomy
. . . finally, feeling despair and no hopelessness

Signs of becoming polarized on the Theoretical Thinking Strength

Continuing to imagine possibilities . . . imagine possibilities . . . imagine possibilities
. . . seeing the pot of gold at the end of the rainbow
. . . being eager to try something new
. . . disregarding facts
. . . having unbridled optimism
. . . finally, living in a dream world

Signs of becoming polarized on the Out-dependent Risking Strength

Continuing to depend on others . . . depend on others . . . depend on others
. . . experiencing a build-up of support and approval of others
. . . saying "yes" when should say "no"
. . . becoming less and less responsible
. . . losing self-confidence
. . . losing the respect of others
. . . finally, losing support and approval of others

Signs of becoming polarized on the Independent Risking Strength

Continuing to depend on self . . . depend on self . . . depend on self

. . . experiencing a build-up of ego and self-importance

. . . talking when should be listening

. . . assuming more and more responsibility

. . . losing confidence in others

. . . losing the support and approval of others

. . . finally, failing and losing of self-confidence

As you go down the list of phrases under each strength they point to more serious problems. Your objective should be to catch the problem early. When you solve the problem early you avoid more painful and disabling problems.

Breaking Polarization

Robby Robinson is Chief, Office of Organizational and Employee Development in the State of Washington. He is also a highly effective teacher of our seminars. He related the following experience to me.

> I was conducting a seminar on The Thomas Concept for a group of state employees. They worked in an office in southwest Washington. At the end of the first day a participant approached me saying, "Could I have a word with you in private?" I told her I would be glad to talk with her.
>
> She began by giving me a brief overview of her life history. This included an unhappy child-

hood, a failed marriage and her frustration in her present job. She also told me that she had been in therapy for twelve years.

She said that her therapist had tried to convince her that she had value and strengths. But had failed. She said she couldn't accept what her therapist was saying because he used the same words that others had used to label her as "weak" and to "put her down."

She went on to say that as the seminar went along she was hearing the same words. But this time in a different context - a context of strengths and choice. The *Thomas Inventory of Core Strengths* had identified her lead strengths as Thinking, Practical Thinking and Out-dependent Risking. For the first time in her life, she saw these as positive. She said she just wanted to thank me for opening her eyes so she could "see herself."

At the end of the seminar the next day she came up to me again. This time she was smiling and thanking me. She said, "You know, I am going back and really talk to my therapist."

About three months later, she attended an advanced course on The Thomas Concept. I was the teacher. She was vivacious and a very active participant. At the first break, I asked her how she was doing. She smiled at me and said, "I am no longer in therapy and I am applying for a supervisory position." She gave me a knowing grin and said, "It pays to flex." I said that was great and asked her to let me know how the interviews turned out. She called me a month later and told me she had gotten the job.

Five years later, I saw her again during a conference. She came up to me and gave me a hug and said "This stuff works!" As we talked she told me that she had two more promotions, a great relationship with a fine man and was happy in her work. Does it work? At least it did with her.

The woman in Robby's story certainly broke her polarization. Just how she did it, I really don't know. But there is probably a basic process that we all use in our own way. I see it as a six-step process.

First, *become aware* that you are, in fact, polarizing.

You can become aware through the pain and frustration of a problem.

Sometimes others can help. They can bring your attention to the fact that you are polarizing.

Second, identify the strength on which you are polarizing.

Usually we are polarizing on more than one polar strength. What you need to do here is to select only one. Select the one that seems to be giving the most problems.

Third, identify the strength you need to emphasize to solve the problem.

It is the strength opposite the one on which you are polarizing.

Fourth, make a conscious personal choice to express the opposite strength.

Let go of the rewards you are getting from polarizing.

Fifth, shift your attention to the opposite strength. Then identify practical ways to express it.

You have the power to **direct your attention!**

Sixth, change your behavior to actually express the opposite strength.

You have the power to **control your behavior**!

Here is how I used these six steps in solving a recent problem.

A couple of days ago I was stuck in trying to write this chapter on polarization. I found myself thinking. . . and thinking . . . and thinking. I was thinking about all sorts of philosophical ideas

– the nature of evil – where evil comes from – how we get involved in it – how all this relates to time-honored religious concepts – on and on. These thoughts kept rolling around in my head. Finally I realized that I wasn't making any progress. I was stuck – spinning my wheels!

The frustration of not making progress made me aware that I was polarizing.

(This was the *First step*)

I was polarizing on both **Thinking** and **Theoretical thinking**. I selected **Thinking** to work on.

(This was the *Second step*)

Its' **opposite strength** is **Risking** so that's what I needed to emphasize. I needed to get into action – do something.

(This was the *Third step*)

Next, I made a conscious **choice** to give up the "fun" I was having in thinking.

(This was the *Fourth step*)

After making my choice, I **shifted my attention** to the **Risking** strength. It seemed to me that the best way to get into action was to start writing. Just go ahead and write something, even though I didn't have all the answers.

(This was the *Fifth step*)

Finally, **I actually did some writing**. I just went ahead and put my best thoughts into the computer. (This was the *Sixth step*)

This broke my polarization on the Thinking strength and got me going! Now I have made a good deal of progress and am feeling very productive.

You don't stop using the strength on which you are polarizing. Instead, you give up the rewards you are getting from expressing it. What you are after are the greater rewards that come from expressing **both** strengths. I gave up the fun I was having with thinking by itself. Then I used **both** my thinking and my risking to get a book written.

You can polarize on being yourself. You can get tied up with yourself and forget about the world. When you do this you develop problems with the world.

You can also polarize on being flexible. You can try so hard to adapt that you forget about yourself. When you do this you develop problems with **yourself**.

Here's a story of how I polarized on "Being Myself."

I was leading a Seminar for a group of Bank Executives. At the time I was in the early stages of developing my concepts. In my presentation I was focused on my own thinking, not on my audience. I talked a lot about the concepts that I was trying to get straight in my own head.

I noticed that some particpants appeared to be

bored. Others were trying to stay awake. The problem was that their reactions didn't register on me very strongly. I had some awareness of their reactions, but I really didn't know what to do about it. I just kept holding forth on theory.

As you can imagine, I had a problem. To compound the problem I was only dimly aware of it. Fortunately for me, the CEO approached me after the seminar. He said, "Jay, I like your concepts, but I think you over-kill them. We don't need theory. What we need are practical suggestions on how to solve some of the people problems we are having around here."

Now, this got my attention! I could see the possibility of losing a valued client. Also, if I kept giving seminars in this way I would probably end up talking to empty rooms.

I was over-doing the theory bit. If I didn't do something to correct the situation, I was in real trouble.

To solve my problem I needed to be more practical. I needed to help my participants see how to use the concepts to solve their problems. My focus needed to shift to practical application.

So I moved over to my practical thinking. I gave more examples to illustrate the concepts. At first I didn't do this very well. I didn't feel confident in dealing with practical problems, but I did the best I could.

My seminars got better in spite of my ineptness in giving examples.

Here's a story where I polarized on "Being Flexible."

My first job as a Psychologist was with a firm of Management Psychologists. We did our work in one-on-one counseling sessions. Our work required us to do three things; first, be keenly aware of the person with whom we were consulting; second, stay focused on their practical problems; third, give advice readily.

Without knowing it, I was in a job that called for an emphasis on all three of my **supporting** strengths – not my lead strengths. In other words, the job really didn't fit me. At the time I didn't know myself very well.

I am a Pattern IV. By nature, I am an independent, theoretical thinker. This job required me to be an out-dependent, practical risker. This was the exact opposite of my natural way.

The good thing about the job was that I was required to be flexible. I had to use my **supporting** strengths. The bad thing was that I couldn't be myself. That is, go ahead and lead out with my natural lead strengths.

I was able to adapt to the situation for awhile. But I paid a great price. After about four years, it began to catch up with me. I would dream of going off to the mountains where I could be by myself and think things through. But I couldn't do that. I had a family to support and they were depending on me.

Things kept getting worse. I had to force myself to go to work every morning. After I "got going" and was working with my clients it was ok – I felt energized and effective. But the same thing would happen the next morning – I had to force myself to get going again.

I was in a high-pressure situation and it was compounded by the fact that I couldn't be myself. I had to put up a front every day – day after day. I was polarizing on being flexible.

I was doing well in the job and the pay was good. But personally I was going downhill. I was beginning to suffer physically. I developed a fungus infection in my lungs and was forced to quit work for a couple of months. I was certainly flexible, but I was so flexible it was killing me!

I had to find a way out of the situation. Of course, I thought about resigning my position and finding some other kind of work. But, I felt effective in doing the work and I was making a good living.

I also felt competent in developing new concepts in the field of Psychology. The problem was that my job didn't permit me the time I needed to do it. Gradually I evolved a plan . . . .

The plan was this: I would quit my job and start my own consulting business.

I was generating considerable income. But I was receiving less than half of it for my salary. I had confidence that I could obtain clients of my own and do the work well. This change would allow me to keep all the fees rather than sharing them. By doing this I could maintain the same income level by working half time. I could spend the rest of my time developing my own concepts in psychology.

I quit my job and put my plan into action. This turned my life around. I was still doing the same type of work. But now, consulting only half time, I could be myself the rest of the time. In being myself, I could exercise my lead strengths in doing development work on my own.

I had stumbled onto a solution that allowed me to be myself and be flexible in an alternating way. Now I could give my lead strengths free rein during my own free time. On the other hand, I was forced to use my supporting strengths in my consulting work. I am convinced that being able to do both allowed me to develop The Thomas Concept.

In looking back I can understand what was going on. But I certainly didn't understand it at the time. What I did know was that I was in pain and needed to get some relief. It was the pain that motivated me to find a solution.

This is the key to understanding our approach.

You "grow" and become stronger through an alternating use of your lead and supporting strengths.

As you move forward in using your lead strengths you will, sooner or later, experience some pain. This is a signal that you have gone as far as you can go with that strength. Now you must start using your **supporting** strengths.

You take another step forward by emphasizing your **supporting** strengths. As you do this, sooner or later, you experience the pain that comes from losing yourself. You become a "phony". Now you must be yourself – emphasize your natural lead strengths again.

As you engage in this back and forth action you become **more sensitive** to the pains on both sides. This enables you to catch the problems at an **earlier time**. You **also develop skill** in moving to the opposite side. As a result, you spend less time in the polarization ditches on either side. This gives you more time to spend on the high road – living a healthy and productive life.

Let the power of opposite strengths work within you!

Chapter 6

How Others See You

Oh wad some Power the giftie gie us
To see oursels as ithers see us!
It wad frae monie a blunder free us
An foolish notion.
What airs in dress an' gait wad lea'e us,
An ev'n devotion!

Robert Burns

Up to this point the focus has been inward – looking hard at you. Now it is time to turn our attention outward – to your relationship with the outside world – particularly other people.

The objective of this chapter is to help you become more aware of how others see you. Being aware of how other people are seeing you is important. It helps you see what you need to do to solve your relationship problems.

You show people who you are in three ways: (1) your behavior, (2) your thinking and (3) your attitude.

What Your Behavior Reveals

Behavior is controlled action!

Your thinking provides the control and your risking gives the action. It takes both to produce human behavior. One is just as important as the other.

In your actual behavior one of these strengths is always dominant. When your thinking outweighs your risking you are reserved. When risking is governing you are assertive.

When you express reserved behavior you listen a good deal. You hold your thoughts and feelings inside. There is a lot going on inside, but not much outside.

When you express assertive behavior you take the initiative. You move into action quickly. You usually talk a lot and freely express your thoughts and feelings. There is a lot going on outside.

Appropriate Behavior

Appropriate behavior is situational!

In some situations you need to be reserved. In others, you need to be assertive.

> For example, let's take the situation where you are a teacher. Here you need to take the initiative and be assertive. This is particularly so at the start. As your teaching progresses, there comes a time when you need to be reserved – stop talking and listen. This is the time when your students need to ask questions and express themselves. The time for you to be assertive will reappear as time goes along.

Tendency to be Reserved

(Patterns I, II, III and IV)

If thinking is your lead strength you tend to be reserved. You want time to think before expressing yourself.

Others see you as:

Stable, rational, calm, thoughtful, careful, prudent, logical, discerning, composed

If you continue to think when it's time for action these positives turn sour. Then others may see you as:

Withdrawn, distant, cold, apathetic, uninterested, indecisive, dry, dull, boring, listless

Tendency to be Assertive

(Patterns V, VI, VII and VIII)

If risking is your lead strength you tend to be assertive. You want to get into action and get things done. You want to move and see things happen.

Others see you as:

Dynamic, exciting, stimulating, enthusiastic, vigorous, spirited, exhilarating, zestful, fun-to-be-around

These positives turn negative if you are assertive when

it's time to be reserved. When you do this people may see you as:

Unstable, pushy, loud mouth, over-emotional, invading, threatening, non-stop talk, annoying, nosy, loose-cannon-on-the-deck

What Your Thinking Reveals

You think in two ways – in a practical way and a theoretical way. These two ways of thinking are equally valuable.

Your thinking is such that one way of thinking is always dominant. When your practical thinking is in the foreground you are looking to the past and seeking the facts. You want to know how things really are – not how they could be.

On the other hand, when your theoretical thinking has the upper hand your thinking changes. Now you think about how things could be. Your imagination is active. Concepts and abstract thoughts are at the center of your attention.

You tend to use one of these types of thinking more than the other. If practical thinking is your lead strength, you tend to focus on facts. On the other side, if theoretical thinking is your lead strength, you tend to focus on ideas.

Tendency to Focus on Facts

(Patterns I, II, V and VII)

If you have a lead strength in practical thinking you

keep your feet on the ground. You feel comfortable with the way things are and want to keep them that way.

Others see you as:

Realistic, down-to-earth, problem-centered, practical, steady, pragmatic, businesslike, fact-oriented, having-common-sense

When you get stuck on the practical side others tend to see you in negative ways. They may use some of these terms to describe you:

Unimaginative, negative, rigid, pessimistic, cynical, gloomy, depressing, having-limited-vision, disheartening, resistant-to-change, can't-see-the-forest-for-the-trees

Tendency to Focus on Ideas

(Patterns III, IV, VI and VIII)

If theoretical thinking is your lead strength you look to the future. You like to imagine how things could be. You feel comfortable in the world of ideas.

People see you as:

Optimistic, imaginative, insightful, hopeful, idealistic, scholarly, educated, upbeat, perceptive

If you stay theoretical when it's time to be practical

others see you in negative ways. They may describe you as:

Impractical, naive, highbrow, dreamer, out-of-touch, incurable optimist, unrealistic, far-out, weird, egghead, bookworm

What your Attitude Reveals

Attitude has to do with how we value things. If we have a "good attitude" towards our work it means we value our work – feel good about it. Conversely, if we have a "bad attitude" it means that we don't value it – we don't like our work.

Your attitude towards others is also a valuing thing. It is how you value yourself compared to others.

Our concern here is how others perceive your attitude towards them. They may think that you value yourself more than you do them. On the other hand, they may think that you value them more than you do yourself.

Tendency to Value Yourself

(Patterns II, IV, VII and VIII)

If in-dependent risking is your lead strength you value yourself. You go your own way. You feel a good deal of self-confidence. You keep focused on your own goals. You follow your own convictions. When you are being yourself people see you as:

self-assured, strong, determined, self-reliant, resolute, self-sufficient, independent, confident, poised, capable

Others may perceive that you value yourself more than you do them. If so, they see you in negative ways. They may describe you as:

selfish, greedy, egotistical, self-seeking, arrogant, conceited, contemptuous, stuck-up, snob, condescending

If in-dependence is your lead strength others may see you as having an "Attitude of Superiority." This can happen even though you are not aware of it.

Here is a personal example:

In my early teenage years a friend said to me, "Jay, you're conceited." I was shocked and as I recall didn't make a response. I hardly knew what the term meant, but I knew it was a negative.

I had no idea that I was communicating this attitude. I didn't feel superior at all. But somehow I was giving this impression to my friend.

Tendency to Value Others

(Patterns I, III, V and VI)

If Out-dependent risking is your lead strength you value other people. You value your relationships highly. You seek to be with people. You like people and others feel comfortable with you.

When you are being yourself others see you as:

warm, accepting, compassionate, caring, helpful, gracious, forgiving, kind, gentle, easy-to-get-along-with

Others may perceive that you value them more than you do yourself. They may use these terms to describe you:

weak, easily-led, wimpy, smothering, docile, meek, submissive, timid, lacks-confidence, faint-of-heart

When you value others more than yourself you may give a false impression. Others may see you as having an "Attitude of Inferiority". You may not feel inferior at all, but the impression can be there.

Chapter 7

Solving Relationship Problems

The objective of this chapter is to help you solve your relationship problems. The first thing is to understand the problem – what is actually going on. The next thing is to know what you need to do to solve it. That's about as far as the book can go – you're on your own in actually solving it.

At the outset, let's settle the question about having problems.

Relationship problems are inescapable. We can be sure that in every relationship, sooner or later, we will have problems. Some people want to soften this reality by calling them "challenges." That's fine, but we will just call them "problems".

A relationship involves responsibility on both sides. You have your problems to solve. Other people have their problems to solve. You can't solve their problems. They can't solve yours. Each of you has a part to play in making the relationship work.

You are 100% responsible for 50% of the relationship.

Concentrating on your 50% has three good results:

First, it keeps you working in the area where you have direct control. You avoid wasting time trying to "make" others respond in a particular way.

Second, you show respect for the other person.

Third, you encourage others to work on their problems. By working hard on your problems you motivate them to work on their problems.

Importance of "Being Yourself"

Being yourself helps to build your relationships. When you are "real" you have a distinctive flavoring – a personal charm that is yours alone. When you are authentic you have a "saltiness" about you. This brings spice and dynamism to your relationships. Others feel your "presence."

Importance of "Being Flexible"

You also need to be flexible in your relationships. You are flexible when you do whatever it takes to make the relationship work. You pay close attention to other people – who they are and where they are coming from. You use the strengths it takes to solve the problem, regardless of your pattern.

Here's a story that tells about a relationship in which the problems were solved.

Dick Murray and I had a working relationship. We were training Pastors to conduct our Seminar. Dick taught at Perkins School of Theology. I was the originator of the seminar.

Dick was a Pattern VII. He was very aggressive, self-confident and came on strong. As a Pattern IV, I tended to do the opposite – be reserved and thoughtful. Dick wanted to move on and get into action. I wanted to hold back and think about it.

Our natural tendencies caused problems. One day Dick got fed-up with my lack of response. He exploded in his typical aggressive way. He said, "Jay, why don't you say something – you just sit there like a bump on a log. Why don't you at least just say something – anything." Dick was angry and frustrated with my quiet behavior. He let me know it in no uncertain terms.

From my point of view I wanted to think it through before responding. I liked to get my thoughts in order then give a perfected response. Dick wasn't interested in a perfected response. He wanted an interaction.

Well, Dick got my attention with his emotional outburst. It was obvious that I was causing a problem. I don't remember how well I understood what was going on at the time. I do remember making my own emotional response. I said, "Dick you push me too hard. I need more time to think before I respond to you. I wish you would just back off and give me time to think."

We were certainly being ourselves. However, in doing so, both of us were causing problems for the other one.

With this confrontation we began to see what we were doing to cause problems. As a result, we agreed to alter our behaviors. I agreed to respond more quickly – at least say something. Dick agreed to stop pushing so hard and give me more time to respond – even if it meant sitting there and not saying anything.

Getting the problems out on the table was a good thing to do. This was a good first step. The next step was to solve the problems by changing our behaviors. I needed to become more assertive and Dick needed to become more reserved. As each of us worked on our own problem the relationship got better.

The relationship didn't become perfect. We still made our typical mistakes. Dick was still assertive and I was still reserved. The difference was that we became more sensitive to the problems we were causing. So we made our adjustments more quickly.

With practice, we developed more skill in

moving to our supporting strengths. The relationship became much more productive. As a bonus, we both enjoyed it more.

Guidelines for Solving Relationship Problems

These guidelines focus on how to solve the problems you cause. By working on your problems you are doing the best thing to help others solve their problems.

STEP 1

Becoming Aware of the Problem

You can become aware of a problem through personal pain and frustration. When this happens, it is up to you to let the other person know of your pain.

In letting the other person know, keep focused on your pain. Give an "I" message. Such as, "I feel (so and so) when you do or say (so and so)".

You can also become aware by someone else letting you know. It is usually the other person in the relationship. They let you know of their pain.

Discussion of the story:

In the story above Dick took the initiative. I became aware of the problem by him telling me of his frustration. This was a very valuable thing for Dick to do. It got the problem out in the open so we could start dealing with it. It took courage for Dick to initiate this confrontation. But it was the right thing to do.

Sharing my own frustration was also a good thing to do. It made Dick aware of the problem he was causing me.

STEP 2

Identify How You Are Polarizing

Here's how to go about it,

First, ask yourself this question. Is it primarily a thinking problem, a behavior problem or an attitude problem?

You usually find that all three types of problems are present. You need to identify the primary one and attend to it.

Second, identify the strength on which you are polarizing.

Third, answer this question. Are you polarizing on "being yourself" or "being flexible"?

Discussion of the story:

I had a behavior problem. My reserved behavior was giving Dick a problem.

I was polarizing on thinking. I was thinking, thinking, and thinking rather than responding to Dick.

Since thinking is a lead strength for me, I was polariz-

ing on being myself. I needed to be more flexible – move to my supporting strength.

STEP 3

Identify the Strength You Need to Emphasize

Identify the strength that is opposite the one on which you are polarizing. This is the strength you need to emphasize.

Discussion of the story:

I was polarizing on thinking. Its' opposite is risking. So I needed to emphasize my risking strength. It was high time for me to become more interactive with Dick – be more assertive.

STEP 4

Identify the Pattern You Need to Express

If you are polarizing on one of your supporting strengths you need to come home to yourself – express your core pattern.

If you are polarizing on one of your lead strengths you need to express one of your flex-patterns. It is the flex-pattern you express when you emphasize the needed strength.

Discussion of the story:

Since I was polarizing on a lead strength, I was polarizing on being myself. I needed to express one of my flex-patterns.

Since I needed to emphasize my risking strength, I needed to express my flex-pattern VIII.

STEP 5

Develop a Plan of Action

Now that you know what you need to do, you are ready to develop a practical plan to do it. Be as specific as you can about how you are going to do it and when.

Keep in mind that the strength on which you are polarizing still needs to be there. You aren't rejecting this strength. You still affirm its' value. You are simply emphasizing the strength needed in this situation.

Discussion of the story:

Dick and I had agreed upon a time for our next meeting. My plan was to be more assertive during this meeting. I would move into my flex-pattern VIII when appropriate.

I planned to pay closer attention to Dick's reactions. I wanted to pick up on the cues that told me he wanted me to respond.

I didn't want to be a pattern VIII. I still wanted to be myself (a pattern IV), but be more assertive when it was appropriate. Then, and only then, would I shift into my flex-pattern VIII.

I also planned to be more forceful in my responses. I tend to be somewhat studied and controlled when I do respond. So it seemed best for me to raise my voice and be more emotional in my reactions to Dick.

STEP 6

Put Your Plan Into Action

You are likely to feel somewhat anxious as you put your plan to work. It is normal to feel awkward and unsure of yourself when trying something new.

> *Regard your effort as a learning exercise. See it as an experiment. Be curious about the outcome.*

Your chances of improving the relationship are good. You certainly have no guarantee here. The other person is just as responsible as you are for making the relationship work. You do the best you can from your side and you have to let it go at that.

Discussion of the story:

I felt good after completing my plan of action. I knew what I was going to do and this gave me some confidence. I went to my next meeting with Dick in good spirits and with a hopeful attitude.

In the beginning Dick took the initiative as usual. It wasn't long, however, before I got the cue. It was clear that he wanted me to express my opinion. I looked him straight in the eye and said, "Dick, I really haven't had enough time to form an opinion. Give me a little time to think about it and I will let you know what I think."

I talked louder and said my piece more forcefully than I usually do. To my surprise, Dick said, "That's fine, it can wait. We don't need to decide to-day." Then we went on to the next issue.

This interaction was highly positive from both of our perspectives. Dick got what he wanted – a strong response. I got what I wanted – time to think.

The interaction seemed to clear the air. We both relaxed. It was probably the most productive meeting we had ever had. We solved more problems and made more progress than ever before. The meeting energized both of us.

Well, we have come to the end of the chapter and the end of the book. I suggest that you start using the relationship guidelines immediately.

Identify a relationship that you want to improve. Then go right to step 1. Work your way through all the six steps. You may be surprised as to how effective you can be in solving a relationship problem.

Let the power of opposite strengths work its wonders in your relationships!

Where to From Here?

INPSYTE is the internet-based company that markets services and products based on The Thomas Concept. You can find us on the Internet at http://www.inpsyte.com.

Come and visit our website. Obtain the *Thomas Inventory of Core Strengths*. Order books, booklets and research papers. Get information on our Certification Schools and Training Programs.

e-mail:
info@inpsyte.com.

Toll-free voice phone in the United States and Canada:
1-888/878-3735

Voice phone in Austin, Texas:
512/327-2656

U. S. Mail:
INPSYTE, P. O. Box 160220, Austin, TX 78716-0220